CW01301658

Famous Donkeys of the Bible

Six Studies for Individuals or Groups

Brant D. Baker

Aesop's fable

A grandfather and his grandson were making their way into town with a donkey. The young boy was riding while his grandfather walked along beside.

Someone muttered, "Look at that -- the little boy is so self-centered he makes his grandfather walk." So they traded places.

Another shouted, "I can't believe you are making that little boy walk - he is so young." So they both mounted the donkey at the edge of town.

Someone else hurled another criticism, "I can't believe your incredible disrespect and cruelty toward the donkey in making him strain under the heavy weight of both of you."

So they walked into town carrying the donkey.

©Brant D. Baker, 2014
ISBN-13: 978-1502329301
ISBN-10: 1502329301

All Scripture is from the New Revised Standard Version of the Bible unless otherwise noted.

Introduction

My wife has developed an odd affection for animals with long ears and soulful faces, a fact that has me wondering if she somehow sees me in the same way. In particular, an interest in donkeys seems to have begun when we returned to the southwest to live, and was aggravated by a tour of the great western national parks our family took in 2005. So fond is she that our children arranged to adopt a donkey as a Christmas gift for their mother. Thankfully our neighborhood covenants disallow livestock, but our daughter found a registered sanctuary in England where donkeys are used with special needs children (www.thedonkeysanctuary.org).

The literature that came with the photo of our adopted donkey, whose name—I am not making this up—is "Moses," tells that the mules of the Emperor Nero had shoes made of silver. Apparently his wife, the Empress Papiya, liked to bathe in donkey's milk and kept 500 silver-shoed females for that purpose.

These tidbits got me musing about some of the famous donkeys in the Bible. Depending on what translation one prefers, there are at least seventy references to the beast in question as either an ass or a donkey, and a number of other inferred references (for example, in the Parable of the Good Samaritan, it is probable that the priest is understood to be riding this common means of transportation and so to have had opportunity to render assistance).

The Bible makes use of donkeys in both the literal and figurative ways. So, for example, an angel of the Lord tells Hagar that the son she carries by the patriarch Abram will be "a wild ass of a man, with his hand against everyone, and everyone's hand against him; and he shall live at odds with all his kin" (Genesis 16:12). Similarly one of Abraham's grandsons, Issachar, is said to be "a strong donkey, lying down between the sheepfolds..." (Genesis 49:14).

Donkeys rate mention in the Ten Commandments (Exodus 20:17), and the prophet Jeremiah makes an unfavorable comparison between the fickle Israel and a female donkey in heat (Jeremiah 2:24), and Ezekiel has even less flattering things to say in a similar vein (Ezekiel 23:19-20).

In the wisdom literature there is an interesting comment made by Zophar in his conversation with Job:

> "Can you find out the deep things of God?
> Can you find out the limit of the Almighty?
> It is higher than heaven—what can you do?
> Deeper than Sheol—what can you know?
> Its measure is longer than the earth,
> and broader than the sea.
> If he passes through, and imprisons,
> and assembles for judgment, who can hinder him?
> For he knows those who are worthless;
> when he sees iniquity, will he not consider it?
> But a stupid person will get understanding,
> when a wild ass is born human (Job 11:7-12).

The Hebrew here is uncertain but the inference seems to be that there are some hopelessly donkey-like people, a sentiment echoes perhaps in Proverbs 26:3 which says, "A whip for the horse, a bridle for the donkey, and a rod for the back of fools."

Hard-headed, foolish donkeys represent some of what we'll look at in this study: those famous human asses in the Bible who either miss or resist the invitation to follow and serve God. These include Balaam, some 1000 Philistines, a man named Nabal (not treated in this study, but you can find his story in 1 Samuel 25), and the priest in the Parable of the Good Samaritan. Then there are those whose lives might be said to represent the better qualities of donkeys—people like Abraham, Jesse, Joseph, and Jesus himself—who were found to be dependable, burden bearing, long suffering, humble, and submissive. There's no particular glory in it, but being this kind of donkey is part of our calling, as we, like that little Palm Sunday beast, bear Christ into the world.

Contents

Abraham's Long Walk
Genesis 22:1-5
~11~

Balaam's Bray
Numbers 22:22-35
~17~

The Jawbone of an Ass
Judges 15:9-17
~25~

The Conflicted Priest
Luke 10:25-37
~31~

Away in a Manger
Luke 2:1-7
~37~

Be A Donkey
Matthew 21:1-17
~43~

Abraham's Long Walk

DISCUSS/REFLECT
What is the longest walk or hike you've ever attempted? Why did you want to go that far? Any interesting stories from that experience?

READ
Genesis 22:1-5

DISCUSS/REFLECT
What questions does this passage raise for you?

READ
God telling Abraham to sacrifice his only son on Mt. Moriah has to be one of the more disturbing stories in the Bible. There are dark remnants of child sacrifice even as there are dark forebodings of God's own supreme sacrifice for our sins. Us? We're just here to talk about donkeys.

As an aside, Abraham, like many of the so-called biblical saints, is a man who at times exhibited donkey-like qualities. At an earlier time in his life, he all but abandoned his wife, the would-be mother of the chosen people, to an admiring Pharaoh. At another time, he went along with an inferior "Plan B" to utilize his wife's maid, Hagar, as a surrogate mother for the great nation that had been promised by God. But let's assign those to a younger Abraham, and for the purpose of this study focus on the donkey itself, and in particular one aspect of a donkey's character that we would all do well to mimic: the trait of dependability and surefootedness in walking long trails.

The text tells us that upon receiving God's instruction, Abraham rose early, *saddled his donkey*, and took Isaac and two young men, plus wood for the burnt offering, and set out for the place that God had shown him. It was apparently no short journey, for "On the third day Abraham looked up and saw the place far away" (Genesis 22:4), which suggests that they still had a ways to go.

Mt. Moriah itself isn't that rugged a challenge. It is traditionally associated with the Temple Mount in Jerusalem because the book of 2 Chronicles reports that the location of Araunah's threshing floor is in Mount Moriah, and that the Temple of Solomon was built over it. (Other scholarship, favoring a Samaritan point of view, identifies Moriah as Mount Gerizim, but this argument doesn't seem as strong.) In truth Mount Moriah is more a ridge than a single peak, none of it over 2500 feet high.

No, the real issue here isn't the physical exertion, although that is not to be overlooked. The key thing, as noted by Leon Kass in his insightful reading of Genesis, is that Abraham and his donkey just kept putting one foot in front of the other. What Abraham (or the donkey) might be thinking isn't given to us, says Kass, because the Genesis narrative "is more concerned with deeds than words, with actions than with beliefs—not because inner life doesn't matter, but because true character is best displayed in action (Leon R. Kass, *The Beginning of Wisdom*, 339).

Jesus says "you will know them by their fruits," which is pretty much the same thing (Matthew 7:20), and James elaborates even further saying, "Was not our ancestor Abraham justified by works when he offered his son Isaac on the altar? You see that faith was active along with his works, and faith was brought to completion by the works... For just as the body without the spirit is dead, so faith without works is also dead" (James 2:21-22, 26).

DISCUSS/REFLECT

Can you think of times when you have walked faithfully on, even though you didn't feel like it? What lessons have you learned about "putting one foot in front of another" out of faithfulness to Christ? Share these experiences as you are comfortable.

READ

So sometimes the Christian life is simply about doing "fruitful works," whether we feel like it or not, just walking faithfully forward. As it turns out, metaphors of walking fill the New Testament, beginning with the words of Jesus himself who said,

"Walk while you have the light, so that the darkness may not overtake you. If you walk in the darkness, you do not know where you are going" (John 12:35). For the Christian the light that shines in truth—the light that drives out the darkness of fear and deceit, shame and guilt, hopelessness and despair—is the light of Christ.

The imagery of walking seems to have been a favorite of the Apostle Paul, who says that "we have been buried with him by baptism into death, so that, just as Christ was raised from the dead by the glory of the Father, so we too might walk in newness of life" (Romans 6:4). Later in the same letter Paul says we are to walk "not according to the flesh but according to the Spirit" (Romans 8:4). Both references would seem to point to a life-walk that is in tune with the subtle nudges of the Spirit, those almost imperceptible tugs at our bridle meant to keep us walking the path God intends.

As an added guide, we are to walk "according to his commandments..." and "in the truth" (2 John 1:6, 3 John 1:4). Here the emphasis seems to be on paying attention to the pathways that have already been spelled out for us, call it the well-marked trail of Scripture, clearly marked in the Ten Commandments and the teaching of Jesus who came to "fulfill the law."

DISCUSS/REFLECT

What verse or passages of the Bible guide you most in your daily walk with God?

READ

There are lots of interesting walking records. A few years ago my son and I did a rim-to-rim hike of the Grand Canyon: one day, 26 miles, about 15,000 feet in total elevation change, and we were pretty impressed with ourselves. I have since learned that some people do rim-to-rim-to-rim, which of course would double our own accomplishment!

Not to be outdone, the Brits have an End to End Challenge, which takes you from one end of their Island to the other, a total of 1,200 miles. More impressive still is the 2011 hike of Jennifer Pharr Davis over the entire 2,175-miles of the Appalachian Trail, in a record time of 46 days, 11 hours, 20 minutes. That translates to hiking up to 16 hours, and 47 miles, a day. Then there is George Meegan, who for 2,425 days walked from Tierra del Fuego, South America to Prudhoe Bay, Alaska. He came back several years later to conclude his walk to Barrow, and thus walk the entire 19,091 mile length of North and South America. But by far the most impressive hike on record is the one carried out by Arthur Blessitt, who since 1968 has carried a cross in 321 countries and who is listed in the Guinness World Records for the world's longest walk of over 40,698 miles.

    The truth is that all of us face some long walks in our lives. Whether it is first learning to walk, or walking at a commencement, or walking down the aisle, or simply walking as a metaphor of life. In these walks neither distance nor time seem to be the key issue; only that like Abraham and his beast, we too are called to keep walking in our journey of faith. There is an irreducible forwardness to our lives. Even if we try not to move, we are in truth being drawn forward: day after day, week after week, season after season, year after year. The dawn will break over us whether we are sleeping through it or running toward it. The way of the donkey, the way of the Bible, would seem to be that we walk faithfully into each new day, perhaps sometimes briskly and with light step, perhaps sometimes with a weary trudge.

    That sense of inevitable, and faithful, forward movement is perhaps nowhere better expressed than in the old hymn *Onward Christian Soldiers*. It seems people started getting nervous about this old favorite back during the Viet Nam War, and I suppose in that day and time such skittishness is to be forgiven. The imagery of combat, however, comes right out of Scripture. "War" as a metaphor for the Christian life has nothing to do with the ugly armed conflicts of nations, but rather with the spiritual battle in which we are all engaged, as we are reminded in passages such as Ephesians 6 to "[p]ut on the whole armor of God, so that you may be able to stand against the wiles of the devil. For our struggle is not against enemies of blood and flesh, but against the rulers, against the authorities, against the cosmic powers of this present darkness, against the spiritual forces of evil in the heavenly places" (11-12).

But it turns out that *Onward Christian Soldiers* was originally written as a walking song, specifically for children who were walking to church (Ian Bradley, The Book of Hymns, p. 333). Besides the well known chorus are the lesser known verses that speak to the spiritual battle of our lives, and which summon God's people ever forward into each new dawn, "Onward then, ye people, join our happy throng, blend with ours your voices in the triumph song. Glory, laud, and honor unto Christ the King, this through countless ages men and angels sing...onward Christian soldiers and donkeys alike.

DISCUSS/REFLECT

In what ways does "walking" as a metaphor for the Christian life work for you? How does it aptly describe a genuine aspect of faithfulness for you?

PRAYER

Pray together as a group for one another in your usual manner. To close, pray out loud together these words:

> *Onward then, ye people, join our happy throng,*
> *blend with ours your voices in the triumph song.*
> *Glory, laud, and honor unto Christ the King,*
> *this through countless ages men and angels sing!*
>
> *Onward Christian soldiers, marching as to war,*
> *with the cross of Jesus, going on before.*

Balaam's Bray

DISCUSS/REFLECT

As far as you know, have you ever received a God-given warning or word? Explain.

READ

Numbers 22:22-35

DISCUSS/REFLECT

What questions does this passage raise for you?

READ

Balak was scared. The Moabite king had seen the Israelite horde camped on the plains across the Jordan from Jericho, and he, along with his people, was in dread. "This horde will now lick up all that is around us, as an ox licks up the grass of the field," Balak said to his council. The king then launched a sure-fire plan: hire the Mesopotamian diviner Balaam to come and put a curse on the Israelites so that he could then defeat them and drive them from his land. So, he sent messengers to make the request (Numbers 22:5-6).

But it seems the request was rejected because the next thing we know, another group is being sent, this time of elders from both Moab and Midian, who take with them the fees for divination as an added incentive (22:7). Balaam seeks the Lord, perhaps for the second time, and the Lord tells him not to go, perhaps for the second time, and so he doesn't. King Balak, of course, is not happy with this result so he sends a third delegation, more numerous and distinguished than the last, who implore Balaam to come and do what the king is wanting done. Balaam replies, "Although Balak were to give me his house full of silver and gold, I could not go beyond the command of the Lord my God, to do less or more..." (22:18). But then, somewhat incomprehensively, Balaam offers to go seek the Lord again. This time the Lord says, "If the men have come to summon you, get up and go with them; but do only what I tell you to do."

It's a little hard to sort out what kind of man Balaam was. Did he follow Yahweh or did he listen to whatever god might speak to him in the moment? Did he truly want to do God's bidding or was he "open" to whatever god, or a man's silver, might lead him to do? These questions never really find resolution in the story, and in fact, there are such obvious tensions in that narrative that many scholars believe two different accounts have been woven together, one favorably inclined toward Balaam and the other not-so-much.

That tension is seen in what follows immediately after God gives Balaam permission to go. No sooner had Balaam saddled his donkey than we are told "God's anger was kindled because he was going, and the angel of the Lord took his stand in the road as his adversary" (22:22). How on earth are we to understand this after God just told Balaam to go?

A couple of ideas come to mind. The first is that God's permission to Balaam was a bit weary. It's not too hard to imagine God like the parent whose teenager keeps asking for permission to go to the party, and who finally just says, "whatever," but who is actually a bit steamed as the car backs down the driveway.

This solution might be guilty of assigning to God some of the pettiness of human emotion, and so I'm more drawn to another explanation, one suggested by the angel's later description of Balaam as "perverse" (vs. 32). The original Hebrew word *yarat* is uncertain at this point. It comes from a primitive root that means to be rash or to rush headlong, and in Latin, to face the wrong way. To be *perverse* is to willfully decide to do the opposite of what is expected or hoped, it is to turn away from what is right and obstinately choose what is wrong. In other words, Balaam seems to be one of those people, like a lot of us, who wants to do what is good and right in one part of himself, but who in another part of himself is opportunistic, greedy and manipulating. I can imagine Balaam, as he saddles his donkey, stubbornly thinking about how he can still have his cake, or perhaps his silver, appearing to do God's will on the one hand, but secretly scheming as to how he might manage to bring down some kind of curse on Israel and therefore get paid a handsome sum for his trip.

DISCUSS/REFLECT

Where have you seen this kind of two-faced "perversity" at work in the world in recent weeks?

READ

As it happens this idea of *stubbornness* is also connected to the obscure Hebrew *yarat*, through the word *mowrat*, which means to be obstinate. Going in that direction makes this whole episode with the donkey a bit of a play on this idea of stubbornness, a character trait we sometimes assign to donkeys, but which is clearly at work in the less attractive parts of our human nature more often than we might want to admit. And, in fairness to donkeys, what is often assigned to them as stubbornness is possibly more the result of caution. A donkey, like most animals, tries to avoid danger, and so will look and think before taking a step in new territory. They only walk where they think it is safe (http:// therealowner.com/pet-stories/are-donkeys-really-stubborn/).

Humans may have similar qualities toward self-preservation, but let's face it, we're often more stubborn than careful. *Three times*, it seems, Balak stubbornly implored Balaam to come, and *three times*, we assume, Balaam stubbornly sought permission to go, asking God for direction until God said what Balaam wanted to hear. And now, just in case we don't get what's happening, there is a donkey, that universal symbol of stubbornness, *three times* refusing to take Balaam where he intends to go.

First the donkey sees the angel standing in the road and turns aside into the field, whereupon Balaam strikes the poor thing to get it back on track. Then the donkey finds itself on a narrow path with a wall on either side, and driven by its fear of the whip, but equally fearful of the angel, it tries to squeeze past, scraping Balaam's foot against the wall, and thereby getting another beating. Finally the angel appears in a narrow place on the path, and left with no way out, the donkey simply lays down and refuses to move. Balaam's anger was kindled, the text says, and he strikes the donkey, this time with his staff—a much more stout instrument than either a heel or a whip—and at that, the Lord opens the mouth of this hapless beast.

"What have I done to you, that you have struck me these three times?"

Balaam, apparently not finding it odd to converse with a donkey, replies, "Because you have made a fool of me… (or, if we could be permitted a more coarse translation, "Because you have made an ass of me…"). I wish I had a sword in my hand! I would kill you right now!"

But the donkey, who apparently also didn't think it odd to be having a conversation with another of its own kind, said to Balaam, "Am I not your donkey, which you have ridden all your life to this day? Have I been in the habit of treating you this way?"

Before we get to what happened next, let's talk about *three things*.

First, I can confirm that the average lifespan of a donkey is 25-30 years, so it is quite probable that this donkey has been ridden by Balaam his whole life.

Second, I can also confirm that animals have the ability to sense things that humans don't. There's nothing mystical about this ability, it's just that animals have a better ability to hear, smell, and sense vibrations than we do. Most of us know about dogs that can warn people of an impending epileptic seizure. How they do this still isn't that well understood, but it may be that the dogs detect subtle changes in behavior or scent before a seizure occurs (www.news.nationalgeographic.com/news/2003/04/04).

Finally, on the question of a talking donkey, I remain neutral. Do I believe God could cause this to happen? Absolutely! Do we need to believe this literally happened for the story to have truth?

Probably not. The Bible is full of parables and other stories that use whimsical literary devices to make their impression on us.

DISCUSS/REFLECT

What other Bible stories can you think of that come to us in a similar way? Do you take such stories literally, or can you find truth in them in other ways?

READ

So, back to Balaam. God apparently wants to make sure, by some dramatic display, that Balaam gets the message he has already received, "Go on your way, but do and say only what God says to do and say."

Balaam finds Balak, and if anyone should get the donkey award, it's the king. Balak first takes Balaam to Ba-moth-baal, literally, *the high places of Baal*, which is significant since this is clearly a showdown between Yahweh and the Canaanite fertility god.

Once there Balaam has Balak build seven altars and together they make an offering of a bull and a ram on each. Then Balaam tells Balak to stay put while he goes to inquire of Yahweh, who in turn puts a word in Balaam's mouth, perhaps a bit reminiscent of the word put into the mouth of the donkey. The word is basically that Balaam can't curse those whom God has blessed. Balak is not pleased and so next takes Balaam to the top of Mount Pisgah, which incidentally is the mountain where God took Moses to look into the Promised Land before he died. There the entire sequence is acted out again—build seven altars, sacrifice a pair of rams and bulls on each, Balaam going to meet Yahweh, Balaam reporting to Balak that he can't say anything against the Israelites, Balak getting angry.

Then, you guessed it, there is a third and final show of stubbornness as King Balak takes Balaam to the top of Mount Peor, which is another cult center for the worship of Baal. Seven more altars and fourteen more sacrifices, but this time Balaam doesn't go and seek the word of the Lord because he already knows it. He gives a lengthy oracle that blesses the socks off of the Israelites. Echoing earlier events, the text tells us that "Balak's anger was kindled against Balaam," but since he couldn't strike the prophet, "he struck his hands together" (24:10). They exchange a few more unhappy words and then part company.

Three acts of stubbornness from Balaam, three from a donkey, and three from Balak. What three lessons can we learn?

> First, from Balaam perhaps we learn something about being pure in heart. Whatever the nature of his *perversity*, it seems God had to get his attention before proceeding. The Danish philosopher Sören Kierkegaard wrote a book entitled, "Purity of Heart Is to Will One Thing," which perfectly summarizes its message. To put it another way, we must strive to be laser focused in following the will of God. When we mix our motives, as possibly Balaam tried to do, we may end up facing God's wrath, as Balaam did.

> Second, from the donkey we might learn that God is stubborn as well. God says what is meant and means what is said, as evidenced in a later oracle from Balaam, "God is not a human being, that he should lie, or a mortal, that he should change his mind. Has he promised, and will he not do it? Has he spoken, and will he not fulfill it?" (23:19). God will not be pestered or persuaded to change what is God's perfect plan. We are to "seek the Lord" in prayer and make our requests known, but then to rest when God's way becomes known.

> And finally, perhaps from Balak we can learn that even our repeated disobedience cannot thwart what God is up to. Balak finally notices this himself when he says, "I summoned you to curse my enemies, but instead you have blessed them these three times. Now be off with you! (24:10). Three times Balak intended evil toward Israel, and three times God used that evil for good (see Genesis 50:20). God is sovereign

and God is good. God is about the work of redemption and resurrection, bringing good from evil and life from death. In this the true power of God is made known to each and every donkey in the world!

DISCUSS/REFLECT

1) In what ways or aspects of life are you a stubborn donkey?

2) With whom do you relate most in the story and why?

3) Which of the three lessons of the story speak most to you and why?

PRAYER

Prayer aloud together:

> I am stubborn, Lord
> You know this about me.
> I am hard headed.
> I am dumb.
> I am always trying
> To get back to the barn.
>
> Forgive me, Lord
> And give me the purity of heart
> To will one thing.

(Adapted from http://yestoprayer.blogspot.com/2007/02/donkey-prayer.html)

The Jawbone of an Ass

DISCUSS/REFLECT
As a group try to remember as much as you can about the story of Samson (no peeking!)

READ
Judges 15:9-17

DISCUSS/REFLECT
What questions does this passage raise for you?

READ
Most fairly literate Christians will know there is a story in the Bible about Samson and Delilah, even if the details are lost. As it turns out Delilah is at least the third woman in Samson's life, as spelled out in a rather colorful story that spills across four chapters of the Book of Judges (13-17). This is because Samson was a judge over Israel for twenty years, a kind of tragic, feet-of-clay, everyday hero of the sort we tend to find in the Bible.

Samson was born to Manoah and his wife during troubled times. As was their repeated habit, the Israelites "did what was evil in the sight of the Lord," and so God had given them into the hand of the Philistines (Judges 13:1). Manoah's wife had been barren, but in a story that echoes across several others, an angel of the Lord appeared and told her to be careful to avoid wine or unclean foods because she was to "conceive and bear a son. No razor is to come on his head," the angel continued, "for the boy shall be a nazirite to God from birth. It is he who shall begin to deliver Israel from the hand of the Philistines" (13:4-5). The life of a nazirite is spelled out in Numbers 6:1-21. It basically involves abstinence from anything related to grapes (especially wine), leaving the hair uncut, and avoidance of a corpse. All of these conditions Samson will manage to violate over the course of his life.

As indicated, Samson's "fatal flaw" seems to have been the fairer sex. One day while on a short journey he spotted a Philistine woman and declared his intention to take her as his wife. This would have violated custom and at best been a second-class kind of marriage, but as the story unfolds, we learn that even this will be used to accomplish God's purposes. We shouldn't construe Samson's rash action as permission for us to do whatever we want, but rather understand that God has the power to redeem our folly.

In this case Samson's folly leads to some unhappy issues with the extended family. As an act of retaliatory justice, Samson destroys the Philistine grain harvest by tying torches to the tails of 300 foxes, which in turn had been tied together in pairs, thus assuring that they would run through the fields in a way so as to do maximum damage. This unfortunately (if perhaps expectedly) led the Philistines to seek their own revenge, burning Samson's wife and her father. In a predictable escalation, Samson then lashes out even more, slaughtering those involved, and by then the cycle of vengeance is in full swing. A large war party of Philistines next makes a raid on a town in Judah, demanding that the people there hand Samson over. In response, the people go to apprehend Samson, who allows himself to be bound and turned over to his enemies (Judges 15:1-13).

Now, up to this point in the Samson saga there has only been a hint of his strength (he had previously torn a lion apart barehanded). At this juncture, however, bound by two new ropes, Samson nonetheless breaks free, the ropes practically melting off of him. Without a weapon Samson improvises, finding the fresh jawbone of a donkey, which he then uses to kill a thousand men (13:15).

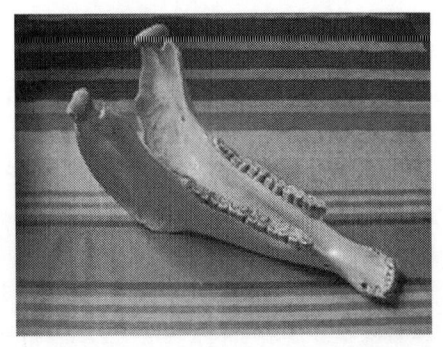

The jawbone of a donkey would be an effective weapon. If gripped by the tooth end it could be a two-headed club, or if broken in half it could become two rather stout and potentially sharp clubs. There is archeological evidence suggesting that donkey jaws were used to create early sickles, perhaps by sharpening the ridge holding the teeth (www.ancientromangoods.com/tech/sickles). Either way, a strong man, filled with the spirit of the Lord, wielding such a weapon, would be formidable indeed.

In taking up this weapon, Samson might have been showing the donkey-like trait of self-defense. In some cultures, donkeys are kept as guard animals to protect livestock against coyotes and stray dogs, as they have a particular dislike for unfamiliar canines. Donkeys are usually gentle animals but when provoked or threatened they can bite, strike with the front hooves, and of course, kick. An angry or protective donkey is a true force of nature, and a donkey's kick can deliver enough force to kill. (http://therealowner. com/pet-stories/are-donkeys-really-stubborn/).

At the end of the day, Samson kills a thousand men with his jawbone weapon. In Hebrew the word *chamar* can mean either donkey or heap, and so Samson (who seems to favor puns and riddles) spins a little wordplay, saying that with the jawbone of a donkey (*chamar*) he has made a heap (*chamar*) of men. The name of the place also derives from this bloody event, The Hill of the Jawbone.

DISCUSS/REFLECT

We've noted that Samson was a kind of tragic, feet-of-clay, everyday hero of the sort we tend to find in the Bible. What other Bible "heroes" of this sort can you think of? What other examples can you think of, either in the Bible or in contemporary life, where God seemed to redeem someone's folly (or outright sin) and use it to God's own purposes?

READ

As we have said, this whole episode is for Samson a matter of enraged justice. We see this theme of righteous anger directed toward an enemy continue in Samson's life up until the very last. We are told that he judged Israel for twenty years (15:20), and then it seems his woman troubles flared up again. He first visits a prostitute in Gaza, which becomes an occasion for his enemies to trap Samson, only to have him escape by tearing out the entire city gate and carting it away. "After this," we learn, "he fell in love with a woman in the valley of Sorek, whose name was Delilah (16:4). Delilah turns out to be a tool of the Philistines, who offer to pay her if she can discover the source of Samson's great strength. After several false tries, which you would think might have tipped Samson off as to Delilah's true intention, she finally nags and pesters him enough that he tells his secret: a razor has never come to his head as part of the nazirite vow made by his mother. Delilah waits until Samson falls asleep on her lap and then calls a man to cut the seven locks from Samson's head. The Philistines seize him, gouge out his eyes, shackle him, and put him to work at the grinding mill: a sad and tired donkey of a man, turning round and round in never-ending circles.

But as is ever the case in God's kingdom, new growth begins, in this case the growth of Samson's hair. Shortly the lords of the Philistines hold a great sacrifice to their god Dagon. "Our god has given Samson our enemy into our hands," they say, and with much merriment they call for Samson to be brought out for their entertainment. Samson is made to stand between the pillars of the great hall, filled with 3000 lords and ladies of the Philistines. And as he is mocked Samson prays, "Lord God, remember me and strengthen me only this once, O God, so that with this one act of revenge I may pay back the Philistines for my two eyes." Then, pushing against the two middle pillars of the building, Samson, who liked puns so much, brought down the house and really killed his audience! And so, we are told, "those he killed at his death were more than those he had killed during his life" (Judges 16:22-31).

DISCUSS/REFLECT

A lot of people get killed in the Old Testament. What explanations of this kind of "holy vengeance" have you heard over the years? In what ways do these various theories work (or not) to harmonize what happened then with the message of Jesus?

READ

There is the possibility that certain features of the Samson stories are exaggerated, as tends to happen with larger-than-life heroes of every age. That one man could kill a thousand other men with *any* type of weapon strains credulity, as does the notion that Samson could kill a lion with his bare hands, or catch and tie together the tails of 300 foxes. To be sure, with God all things are possible, so all of these things surely *could* have happened just this way. But I think that because God politely refuses to demand our belief, there is always room for doubt in the biblical stories.

Happily the Bible doesn't require that we believe Samson killed 1000 men, or captured 300 foxes, in order for us to still receive its saving truth. And the saving truth of this story seems to be that God can use flawed people to accomplish divine purposes.

Samson is at best a failed hero. He has repeatedly violated his nazirite vow and yet "the spirit of the Lord" *rushes* on him (14:5, 14:19, 15:14) and he is able to do amazing things "to begin to deliver Israel from the hand of the Philistines" (13:5).

Samson's tragic end is surely not what God had in mind from the start. Samson's life could probably have been lived out another way. As noted, God has the to redeem our folly, but sometimes God uses our folly to God's own purposes without redeeming it at all. Actions have consequences, and in Samson's case his folly does finally seem to be unredeemed, as he blindly refuses to see Delilah's treachery. His death is tragic, but even that accomplishes God's deliverance of Israel from the hated Philistines.

And so we need to be very careful here: when we say that God can use flawed people to accomplish divine purposes, we are not suggesting that we simply celebrate our imperfections. The complimentary messages of the Christian faith are that we are loved, accepted, and forgiven by God's grace as expressed to us in Jesus Christ, *and* that we are therefore free to grow and change, unburdened by guilt and sin, thus living into God's preferred plan and purpose for our lives.

The Bible is filled with encouragements that we work out our salvation with fear and trembling (Phil 2:12), that we grow up in every way into Christ (Eph 4:15), that we press on toward the goal for the prize of the upward call of God in Christ Jesus (Phil 3:14), that we seek the things that are above (Col 3:1), that we put away our former way of life and be renewed in the spirit of our minds, clothed with a new self created according to the likeness of God in true righteousness and holiness (Eph 4:22-24), that we bear the fruit of the Spirit (Galatians 5:22), that we long for pure, spiritual milk, so that by it we may grow into salvation (1 Pet 2.2), that we grow in the grace and knowledge of our Lord and Savior Jesus Christ (2 Pet 3:18), that we crucify the flesh with its passions and desires (Gal 5.24), and my favorite, that we present our bodies as a living sacrifice, holy and acceptable to God, which is our spiritual worship, not being conformed to this world, but transformed by the renewing of our minds, so that we may discern what is the good and acceptable and perfect will of God (Rom 12:1-2).

There is clearly no room here for complacency or compliance with the status quo, so don't be a jawbone, or a donkey, or even a Samson, and instead grow up in Christ!

DISCUSS/REFLECT

1) What does it mean to say that God politely refuses to demand our belief, and so allows for us to doubt?

2) How do you see people being successful in balancing the love and acceptance of God "just as they are," on the one hand, and the encouragement that we are to "grow up in Christ" on the other?

3) Which of the verses urging the continual improvement to our character resonates most with you, and why?

PRAYER

In an unscripted fashion, have each participant to say aloud the verse from the closing section that they like best, offering it all as a prayer to our Lord.

The Conflicted Priest

DISCUSS/REFLECT
Describe a time when you felt conflicted about what to do, a time when you were able to make good arguments that led in two opposite directions. What did you decide to do, and why?

READ
Luke 10:25-37

DISCUSS/REFLECT
What questions does this passage raise for you?

READ
Jesus was once asked to clarify the definition of "neighbor." In reply he tells the story most of us know so well. "A man was going down from Jerusalem to Jericho and fell into the hands of robbers, who stripped him, beat him, and went away, leaving him half dead. Now by chance a priest was going down that road; and when he saw him, he passed by on the other side" (Luke 10:30-31).

For the purposes of studying famous donkeys of the Bible, this will be far enough. Bible scholar Dr. Kenneth Bailey, who lived and worked in the middle east for decades, notes that the priest in this parable would have been presumed to be riding a donkey. Priests were among the upper classes of their society, and no one with any status would take a seventeen-mile hike through the desert. The poor have to walk, says Bailey, but everyone else, especially the upper classes, always ride. This is the natural assumption of the parable" (*Through Peasant Eyes*, 43).

Bailey strengthens his assertion by making comparison to a farmer who might say, "I'm going into town." If the town is seventeen miles away there is no need to add that he is driving his truck, it is implied. In the mind's eye of Jesus' listeners this detail is assumed, and is given force when later the Samaritan is said to have put the wounded man on his *own* animal. "The parable turns on the presupposition that what the Samaritan *did,* at least the priest *could* have done. If this is not true," says Bailey, "we would be obliged to conclude, 'Of course the Samaritan should help the man; he is the only one who really can.' Rather, the parable assumes an equal potential for service, at least on the part of the priest and the Samaritan" (*Ibid.*).

But how can we know it was a donkey? Well, first, please remember that the whole story is a fiction to begin with. Jesus told the parable to illustrate a point. The encounter never happened, but certainly could have. We are making an assumption about a story, but it is an assumption based on a degree of fact. Donkeys were the dusty old pick-up trucks and family sedans of their day. They were used by laborers, landowners, and merchants alike. Donkeys were used for mundane chores, both in small villages and in big cities. The safest assumption, were the events to have actually taken place, is that a donkey would have been at the center of it, not only under the priest, but under the Samaritan as well.

DISCUSS/REFLECT

Just for fun: what is the most reliable vehicle you ever owned?

READ

We have established that donkeys are cautious creatures. Their reputation for being stubborn probably has more to do with their reluctance to take risks, and in this the priest may have been feeling like a donkey. To be honest, I feel some legitimate compassion for him. The older we get, it seems the more we end up doing risk analysis. I remember taking my young children ice skating when I was in my early forties, and even then I simply assumed that I would be coming home with a broken arm (thankfully I didn't). As we get older we look at things differently, whether it be ice cream (too many calories and perhaps too much dairy?), ladders (maybe we really don't need Christmas lights up on the second story any more...), and investments (a federally insured Certificate of Deposit can sometimes look pretty attractive, the infinitesimally small rate of return notwithstanding!).

A cautious priest, concerned with risk, would have a lot to think about in this situation. First, there's the possibility the man lying beside the road might simply have gotten his just desserts; in other words, if trouble finds you it's probably because you had it coming. Then there would be concern that the man is simply posing as a wounded victim in order to take advantage of a passer-by. Finally, there would be real concern that the man might be dead. If that were the case, then any contact with him would defile the priest, which would in turn impact his ability to carry out his duties, which in turn would have a negative impact on his family, who depend on him for the support he earns through these activities. It turns out that priests were paid through a *wave offering* of grain, a tithe of the tithe, which could only be eaten in a state of ritual purity. Dr. Bailey notes that the priest is struggling with trying to be a good man (Ibid., 44-45). He is bound to love his neighbor, but he doesn't know if the man is, in fact, a fellow Jew (which was the definition of "neighbor") or a Gentile, or dead. He has a lot to think about, but there is still more.

Jesus says the priest is traveling *down* from Jerusalem to Jericho. The inference here is that he has completed his two weeks of temple service and is heading home. But Jerusalem is where he would need to go for any ritual purification that might be necessary from contact with a dead body. That process was not only costly in terms of money but also in terms of time, taking as long as a week. He's been away two weeks already, and now he's heading home; the commandment not to be defiled by a corpse is absolute, while the commandment to love a neighbor is conditioned on knowing that the person in question is a neighbor. Once more, a lot to think about.

In the end the priest is a victim of a rule book ethical system. Life for him was a system of do's and don't's, and he seems to take comfort in simply plodding like a cautious donkey, traveling the same ruts in the road left by others. We are sympathetic to his assessment of the risk, but we wonder if he has found too much security in having a quick, certain answer to all of life's questions. The problem is that the rutted road can suddenly have a needy and perhaps unconscious person sprawled across it. When that happens we might suddenly discover that our primary rule is to maintain the status quo, which seems to be the burden of the priest as he passes by on the other side of the road, deep in his many things to think about.

DISCUSS/REFLECT

In what part of your life are you most cautious and why? Is there any part of your life in which you are less careful?

In what ways do the rules you live by sometimes help you navigate risk? Are there any ways in which those same rules create conflicts for you of the sort faced by the priest?

READ

Those listening to the story Jesus told would not have been surprised to hear that next a Levite was coming down the road, nor that following him would be a third person, presumably a Jewish layman. Like the priests, both Levites and laymen were expected to do two weeks of temple service, so this would have been a normal procession. Further, each would know of the other for any number of reasons. For one, travel on dangerous roads means one would be wise to know who was ahead and behind. For another, this particular road has long sections where a person can see several miles in either direction. The caution of the priest would have been telegraphed back to the Levite, who seeing that the priest had done nothing, would simply follow his lead and pass over the wounded man.

The unexpected twist in the tale, then, is that it is not a Jewish layman, but a Samaritan who is next in line. To be clear, he faces almost all of the same risks as the priest: this could be a set up for robbery, or the man could be dead in which case he would be defiled. If that happened, since Samaritans were not Gentiles but were in fact bound by the same Torah as the others, he would face the same costly and lengthy time of ritual purification. And beyond all that, if the injured man turned out to be Jewish, then what possible motivation would the Samaritan have to render aid at all, especially when the previous two had passed by one of their own? That being said, the Samaritan's main advantage is that as an outsider he is unlikely to be influenced by the actions of either the priest or the Levite before him. He can, as it were, step outside the ruts in the road of those who have gone before him and make a different decision (Ibid., 48-49).

This, of course, is what he does, and the reason is that he feels "compassion." This is a very strong word in Greek, and is based on the word for "innards." In our own vernacular we might say that he had a "gut reaction," feeling so strongly that it was almost a physical sensation demanding he act, and his first action is to give first aid.

A wonderful and subtle detail of the story is that Jesus, in describing the actions of the Samaritan, echoes passages from Jeremiah and Hosea that describe God's same tender care to heal the wounds of Israel. "The symbolism is clear and strong," notes Bailey. God is the one who saves and who chooses agents of salvation, and the agent of salvation in this story is amazingly a Samaritan, a rejected outsider. It is an image that also points us back to Jesus himself (Ibid., 50).

Next the Samaritan puts the injured man on *his own* animal (suggesting he might have had other animals, in which case perhaps suggesting he was a merchant). Bailey notes that the Samaritan's own animal, according to Old Syriac translations, was in fact a donkey (Ibid., 51)! But the verb Jesus uses here could mean either that the Samaritan *brought* the man on his donkey, or that he *led* the donkey with the man on it. If the latter were the case, then Jesus takes the twist in his tale and turns it a bit further. Why? Because there is a *huge* social distinction between riders and those who lead animals in the Middle East. Bailey relates that on numerous occasions he tried to convince a young man who was leading the donkey on which he was riding to ride with him, only to be refused, because from the young man's point of view, that would have been a presumptuous violation of social order. Bailey concludes, "we may have here a case of a middle-class merchant with a number of animals and some goods who takes upon himself the form of a servant and *leads* the donkey to the inn" (Ibid.). Once more, the images of Jesus build: outsider, healer, and now servant.

DISCUSS/REFLECT
Which of these subtle details in the story do you find most attractive or compelling, and why?

READ
The original question was, "Who is my neighbor?" The lawyer who asked finds in Jesus' answer that *everyone* is to be counted as our neighbor. The lawyer was seeking a set of rules to manage life and its risks, but Jesus lets him know that compassion is the only rule we have. And compassion, it turns out, is frequently messy, often inconvenient, and usually hurts deep down in our gut.
Still, it is God's way. I don't pretend to understand this, but it is my observation that suffering love seems to be what works in this world God has made. Suffering love, besides what it does to tear down our pride and build up our character, is the high and noble price that when paid, removes the curse and empowers healing.

DISCUSS/REFLECT
Is there an area of your life, or a relationship, in which God might be calling you to show "suffering love?" What exactly would that look like for you?

PRAYER
Designate someone to pray, or pray openly for one another as you are led, paying special attention to the last question (above).

Away in a Manger

DISCUSS/REFLECT
Are you more of a control-oriented person, or more of a whatever-happens type? Give an example.

READ
Luke 2:1-7

DISCUSS/REFLECT
What questions does this passage raise for you?

READ
Sometimes by design, notes author Jean Blomquist, but more often by default, we distance ourselves from God coming into our lives by our attempts to contain and control what is happening. Happily these efforts don't appear to detain or deter the Divine. And very often it seems God uses humor and hilarity to break through the barriers we construct. A wonderful example of this "breaking through," Blomquist notes, can be seen in a painting by Piero della Francesca (c1415-1492), an Italian artist of the early Renaissance period. In Piero's painting of "The Nativity," we see a ragged stable with a tattered roof, with the players in God's divine drama staged in the foreground (it's worth finding the painting on wikiart.org). Here's how Blomquist describes the scene:

> Dressed in Renaissance garb, five angels, carefully grouped behind the baby Jesus, sing sweetly, accompanied by quiet lutes played by the angels standing at each end. In the background, to the right, are the men--dully solemn and vaguely removed. Standing with them is a solid, brown ox that gazes steadily at the viewer with deep, searching eyes, asking us, perhaps, to open not only our eyes to this sacred scene but our hearts as well. Joseph is seated, turned away from Mary and Jesus, staring off into the distance. Two shepherds stand at his side, one with his arm raised and his

index finger piously pointed toward heaven--just in case we missed the point of what he thinks is going on here.

In the foreground, a stiff-limbed, doll-like Jesus lies on the ground (no manger here), resting on the train of Mary's luminous blue cloak. Mary kneels, prayerfully adoring him. She is elegantly clothed, her face perfectly composed, every hair in place. She has just come, it appears, not from childbirth but from the beauty salon.

All the elements of the painting are tightly controlled, except one. Behind the perfect Madonna, the distracted men, and the sure-footed ox, peeking out from behind the shoulder of an angel, is a donkey. With its head thrown back, mouth wide open, and teeth gleaming, it brays freely and gloriously.

Asks Blomquist, "Why does Piero, whose creative powers had waned and who seemed to have lost his earlier interest in painting, unexpectedly experience a resurgence of his former passion and paint this late masterpiece of the Nativity? And why, in such a carefully orchestrated painting, does he include a brazenly braying donkey?" She continues,

> I cannot know the mind of Piero, but for me this painting speaks delightfully of the unexpected incursion of the Divine, the magnificently mundane manifestations of God, the hilarity of the Holy in our lives--and our amazing ability to remain oblivious to it. Like the figures in this Renaissance painting, we often stand around solemnly, making certain everything and everyone is in order: angel choir over there, shepherds and Joseph over here, Mary right there in front by the baby. Straight out of Manger Management 101, we attempt to orchestrate how God is manifested among us--if not within the confines of a restrictive manger, at least on our carefully arranged coattails.
>
> But then God, or a donkey, or a baby turns things upside down. Over and over the Holy breaks through barriers with a glorious bray and a grace-filled grin. What the donkey sees and understands is what everyone else in the picture seems to have missed: God's upside-down-coming-down-to-be-with-us. What could be more incongruous, less solemn? What could be more wonder-filled than this absolute turning of the world on its head? A tiny, vulnerable infant brings hope, healing, and life to a hopeless, broken and dying world (Jean Blomquist, Weavings v IX, No 6 Nov/Dec 1994).

DISCUSS/REFLECT

What do you enjoy most about Blomquist's reflection on Piero's depiction of the manger scene? Do you agree with her interpretation? Why or why not?

READ

While not specifically mentioned, church tradition does hold that it was a donkey who carried a pregnant Mary from Nazareth to Bethlehem, and then later from Bethlehem to Egypt, and later still, back again. Each was a long journey and it makes sense to imagine that a donkey would be involved, especially for a Mary "great with child." Whether or not that donkey was braying gloriously at the manger, you can decide for yourself, but I think Blomquist is on to something when she assigns to Piero and his donkey an insight into God's glorious and gracious determination to break into our stoic world with joy and wonder.

Meanwhile, on a nearby hillside, an angel chorus is giving a once-in-eternity serenade to a group of frightened shepherds. "Glory to God in the highest heaven," they sing, "and on earth peace among those whom he favors." And who does God favor? Why, those who receive this offer of peace, of course! It's a bit of a circular argument, but essentially God's gift of *shalom* is available to everyone who will take it. God's *shalom* isn't exclusive in any way, except that to know it one must first receive it.

The non-exclusivity of this offer is made clear by the audience. As you may know, shepherds weren't exactly at the top of the social ladder in ancient Israel. Shepherds were simple men who mostly didn't have any other skills. And, unlike the elite scribes and Pharisees of Jerusalem, keeping the ceremonial law wasn't high on the shepherd's to-do list...not much opportunity, or need, for hand washing out in the field! (This is almost ironic when we consider that the sheep for which they were caring there on the hills around Bethlehem were probably headed to the Temple for use in ceremonial and holy ways!)

So let's review: it is to simply, uneducated, and perhaps even uncouth men that the angels make their announcement (not to mention their flocks of sheep who are treated to the concert as well). Meanwhile, back at the manger—the dirty, smelly, crude manger—Mary, Joseph and Jesus are surrounded by animals, including, most probably, a donkey. Angels and donkeys, all proclaiming peace to the most unlikely people in the most unlikely of places.

Not too many of us would be bold enough to identify with angels, even though Psalm 8:5 suggests that we are closer to God than they are! Still, that seems a stretch for us. We're more comfortable thinking of ourselves as the donkeys we know we too often become. But as we've learned in this study so far, donkeys are pretty noble little creatures. We've learned that they are loyal, dependable, burden bearing, long suffering, humble, and submissive. A website called therealowner.com says that donkeys are quite sociable, and that they will often communicate with other donkeys that they can't even see by means of their very loud bray, which can be heard at quite a long distance. Perhaps, then, this is our calling as well. To be like a donkey, braying loudly the Good News of peace for all who will receive it, God's "upside-down-coming-down-to-be-with-us."

DISCUSS/REFLECT

1) To whom can you most relate—the shepherds, the angels, or the donkeys? Why?

2) According to your answer, how are you proclaiming the Good News of God's in-breaking in Jesus Christ? To whom, specifically, are you proclaiming it?

PRAYER

As a group say together "The Prayer of the Donkey," a poem by Carmen Bernos De Gasztold ((1919 - 1995), a sister at the Benedictine Abbeye Saint Louis du Temple.

O God, who made me
to trudge along the road
always,
to carry heavy loads
always,

and to be beaten
always!
Give me great courage and gentleness.
One day let somebody understand me—

that I may no longer want to weep
because I can never say what I mean
and they make fun of me.
Let me find a juicy thistle—

and make them give me time to pick it.
And, Lord, one day, let me find again
my little brother of the Christmas crib.

Amen.

Be A Donkey

DISCUSS/REFLECT
Tell about a time you rode a donkey, or a mule, or a horse. (Do you know the difference?)

READ
Matthew 21:1-17

DISCUSS/REFLECT
What questions does this passage raise for you?

READ
Legend says the cruciform pattern on a donkey's back was put there as a reminder to all that this humble beast was chosen to carry Jesus on Palm Sunday. All three synoptic gospel writers—Matthew, Mark, and Luke—use a Greek word that refers to a young donkey, and Matthew goes even further to link this choice to an Old Testament prophecy:

> "Rejoice greatly, O daughter Zion!
> Shout aloud, O daughter Jerusalem!
> Lo, your king comes to you; triumphant and victorious is he,
> Humble and riding on a donkey, on a colt, the foal of a donkey.
> Zechariah 9:9

The prophecies carry a kind of divine mystery: in those days a king who was victorious and triumphant would come riding a horse, a noble, majestic, and somewhat imposing animal. But the king who came in peace rode a donkey, a much more humble mount. Jesus is sending a very deliberate message to anyone who cares to notice: he rides into Jerusalem triumphant and victorious, but also comes in peace and humility.

Actor Steven Mosely once wrote a short piece on what it must have been like to have been there that day. It must have had a special kind of momentum, he says, as people cured from a whole array of physical and spiritual afflictions found themselves a part of this impromptu parade.

> *Former cripples, leaping as they walked, exulted in their supple limbs. Men born blind gazed wide-eyed at the glorious scenery. Those long bound by demons walked erect and clear-eyed, conversing happily. Men and women shut in for years by deafness now walked fascinated by bird songs, wind in the trees, and Jesus' voice. Former lepers wept for joy at the thought that none of the faces close by in the crowd fled from them in terror. Several who had been dumb couldn't stop shouting praises. Former prostitutes, tax-collectors and others who had crawled out from the underbelly of society followed gladly, knowing they could now live pure lives in the open sun.*

And of course, as part of the procession was the humble beast bearing the King of all Kings, the Lord of all Lords.

Just to be clear, we're talking about donkeys, not mules. A mule is what you get when a donkey is bred to a horse, and as a result mules tend to be a bit larger than donkeys. If the father is the donkey, which is to say a jack, the outcome is a mule, which can be either male or female. If the father is a horse and the mother is a donkey, which is to say a jennet, the outcome is a hinny, which can also be either male or female. Male mules and hinnies are infertile, while female mules and hinnies are fertile but are not often bred.

So, we're talking about donkeys, which are generally loyal and good-natured animals, hard-working servants that carry the burdens of others with sure feet and strong backs. There is an interesting phrase in each of the gospels about the procurement of the donkey used that day. The disciples are instructed to tell the owner, "The Lord needs it." And so it's not hard to imagine that part of the invitation of Palm Sunday is that each and every one of us be a donkey, carrying Christ out into the world. There's no particular glory in it, but it's not hard to imagine that the Lord wants us to be part of his rag-tag parade of newly healed and whole donkeys, ready to do what he asks of us.

DISCUSS/REFLECT
What might it mean for you to humbly bear Christ into the world like that little Palm Sunday donkey?

READ
One way we might bear Christ into the world is by faithfully walking along the twisting, turning path of our lives.

Donkeys have been long favored by travelers as a means of transportation, especially on steep rocky trails. You might think that they use donkeys because their smaller feet and shorter legs make them more stable on the trail; or that some innate intelligence made these creatures more capable of picking out the best track to follow. But according to pastor, theologian, and author Leonard Sweet, almost the exact opposite is the case. Far from being cautious and too reticent to go near the steep edges of the canyon trail, donkeys often scare their passengers to death by walking as close to the edge as possible. Instead of hugging the protected side of the track, the donkeys actually prefer walking the trail right along the very edge of the precipice. It seems that donkeys feel safest and most secure when they can see the edge, when they can know where the greatest danger lies. While it may scare their human passengers, what scares a donkey is knowing an edge is near, but not being able to see it and so gauge the best path to take.

If we are to be donkeys for Christ, we are called to walk in faithfulness, and at some apparent risk. Metaphors of walking fill the New Testament, beginning with the words of Jesus himself who said in John 12, "The light is with you for a little longer. Walk while you have the light, so that the darkness may not overtake you. If you walk in the darkness, you do not know where you are going. While you have the light, believe in the light, so that you may become children of light."

In Romans 8:4 the Apostle Paul, inspired by the Holy Spirit, said, "walk not according to the flesh but according to the Spirit," and in 2 Corinthians 5:7 we read, "...for we walk by faith, not by sight." And finally in the letters of John we read, "And this is love, that we walk according to his commandments... I have no greater joy than this, to hear that my children are walking in the truth" (2 John 1:6, 3 John 1:4).

So to walk like a donkey means to walk knowing where danger lies, it means to walk in the light, to walk in new life, to walk according to the Spirit, to walk according to Christ's commandments, and to walk in the truth.

DISCUSS/REFLECT

Give one specific way in which you can walk with Christ—in the light, or in new life, or according to the Spirit, or according to Christ's commands, or in the truth—in the week ahead.

READ

Another part of being a donkey means carrying heavy loads, and again, the work of bearing and carrying is an essential part of what it means to be a disciple of Christ. Jesus uses the word in a slightly different connotation during his farewell discourse to the twelve during the Last Supper. He says, "My Father is glorified by this, that you bear much fruit and become my disciples...go and bear fruit, fruit that will last, so that the Father will give you whatever you ask him in my name" (John 15:8-9, 16).

When looking at these words we sometimes focus on the issue of "abiding in Christ" and "clinging to the vine," which is certainly a part of it, but abiding and clinging are not ends in themselves. Christ is calling us to bear fruit, and the fruit that will last is the fruit of building the kingdom through changed lives. Men and women are literally dying every day for lack of the fruit we as Christ-followers have to give them, sweet fruit of God's love, God's forgiveness of sin, God's intention for new life for all creation. We are to bear such fruit.

Not only are we to bear fruit as we carry Christ into the world like little Palm Sunday donkeys, but we are also to bear one another in various ways. In Galatians 6:2 we read, "Bear one another's burdens, and in this way you will fulfill the law of Christ." In Ephesians 4 we are admonished to "...lead a life worthy of the calling to which you have been called, with all humility and gentleness, with patience, bearing with one another in love..." (1-2). And in Colossians 3 we are asked to, "Bear with one another and, if anyone has a complaint against another, forgive each other; just as the Lord has forgiven you..." (13).

So, to bear and carry as Christ asks of us means to bear fruit, to bear one another's burdens, to bear one another in love, and to bear another's complaint and forgive.

DISCUSS/REFLECT

Give one specific way in which you will bear and carry Christ—by helping bear someone else's burden, by bearing someone in love, or by bearing a complaint and offering forgiveness—in the week ahead.

READ

Finally, to be a donkey for our Lord means to receive little recognition. If horses were the sports cars of the day, and camels perhaps the Mac trucks, then donkeys were the dusty old pickup necessary for everyday work. They got used by laborers, landowners, and merchants alike. The donkey accomplished the most mundane of daily tasks in small villages and inside the big cities as well. Gray, substantial, and subservient, donkeys were a necessary, but unexceptional, part of first-century life.

Let's face it: little girls don't dream of riding across summer fields on a little donkey. The Kentucky Derby doesn't blow the herald horn for a herd of dinky donkeys to race around the track. Being a donkey isn't what you would call a glamour assignment, and here again, there are many passages that speak of us living our life in Christ with all humility and gentleness, with patience (Ephesians 4:1-2); of clothing ourselves with compassion, kindness, and meekness, patience (Colossians 3:12); of doing nothing from selfish ambition or conceit, but in humility regarding others as better than ourselves (Philippians 2:3-5); and of humbling ourselves under the mighty hand of God, so that he may exalt you in due time (1 Peter 5:6-7).

DISCUSS/REFLECT
Give one specific way in which you will live in greater humility, gentleness, patience, compassion, kindness, and/or meekness in the week ahead.

PRAYER
As a group join hands in a circle and shout as loudly as you can, "Hosanna! Blessed is he who comes in the name of the Lord."
Again!

Other books and studies by Brant Baker

- Hands-On Christianity: Eight Studies for Small Groups
- Wine in the Bible: Eight Studies for Small Groups
- 50 Skills You Need for a Decent Chance of Success
- The Gamer Bible Study: Six Studies for Teens
- The Abingdon Children's Sermon Library (3 vols)(Editor)
- Let the Children Play
- Teaching People to Pray
- The Jesus Story (with Ben Johnson)
- Welcoming the Children
- Let the Children Come

FIND ALL THESE, PLUS NEW PROJECTS AT **www.brantbaker.info**

Printed in Great Britain
by Amazon